Don't Lead Gentle

S.E.Y

BookLeaf Publishing

India | USA | UK

Presentation by *BookLeaf Publishing*

Web: www.bookleafpub.com

E-mail: info@bookleafpub.com

ISBN: 978-93-5744-930-4

First edition 2021

DEDICATION

To Rowan, may we teach you what it means to love, grow, and lead your dreams.

ACKNOWLEDGEMENT

Thank you to my husband, who gives me peace, takes none of my shit, and to whom without I would not have the time to write a single word, leading to my insanity.

PREFACE

This anthology is for those that close their eyes and breathe deeply into the cool nights to find their peace.

One

anything crystalized is
more beautiful.

But I wonder if that's why
my heart
is so
hard.

Two

2

Fill me to the brim.
And watch me pour over.

It may surprise you,
the things that come

from my cauldron.

Three

I have something inside me
that is dark green,
like a black forest.
It's foggy there
some mornings,
just before the rain comes
laying through.
There's an onyx pond
in the center,
where opal eyes stare up.
Within the brush
glistens moonstone.
The soil is fragrant
and warm.
It makes a nice bed
for the mushrooms that grow
luminescent in the darkness.

This forest is my soul,
and here
it is quiet.

Four

You are my every story.

My fantasy of
dragons, swords, and happy endings.

You are embedded in every tale I spin.

In every word.

Five

5

I wish I knew the name

of the demon in my heart.

Six

Confidence is both a look on your face

and a glass sheet
over your

heart.

....

I always have my crown.
Whether it be on my head,
or hanging on the back
of my chair.

....

You may have noticed
that I'm quiet today.

Fear me.

And the Dragon in my
blood.
For today it slumbers,
and tomorrow,
it shall wake.

Seven

7

Let the Darkness tell you stories

you'd be amazed at the things it's seen.

Eight

Their eyes blackened
and staring into the place
between the stars.
That stardust collecting
there
like soot in a fireplace,
twinkling in the eyes
that know time itself by heart.

The knowing of things that should remain
unknown,
that was the beast that dwelled.

9

I put gold leafing
on my tongue.

But now

I can't speak.

Ten

I wish you could see the stains on my skin
for nothing more
than to know
that I have lived.

And I have lived well.

....

Don't touch me.

Today,
I don't want to bleed

into anyone
else.

....

I am both consumed by my heart

and heartless altogether.

....

Be a light in the darkness

they say.

But they never tell you
how hard it is to burn

alone.

....

How amazing to know
I have not cried from sorrow
in such a long time.

Eleven

12

This heart of mine

is too fine for your hands.
I run through your fingers
like soft earth.

Stop tilling me.
I'm trying to grow something.

Twelve

I've yet to decide how this will end.
But I know my start,
every root,
actually.

I've known who I am since I was a child,
staring across foggy fields and knowing their
names.

I've known since the smell of rain washed
across mountains,
and I waited in anticipation for its arrival.

Since the cool of winter came,
and so did my blanket, set to wrap me so I may
play in the chill of ice
and cool blades.

I've known since I was bathed
in the light of oil lamps.

Since I sat with a sister in my lap,
and awaited holidays,
and the homemade dresses it brought.

See, I'm purely homemade.

My happiness, too.

I grew up on the smell of
mountain peeks.
On the scurry of the animals
in the night.
Of monsters just in the shadows,
lurking between the ferns.
I grew up down dirt paths,
and tiny fences made of sticks.
On elk herds,
and cool mornings.

And they wander,
why I am raw.

I've yet to decide how this will end, but
I do know where I'm going.
It's much the same, just
changed.

I'm still waking to that morning and
know the fog.
I still know the names,
of each field around me, but
I am teaching them too.
I hold the hand of a child, that
sits in my lap,
and I spin her happiness.

I make her dresses,
her blankets,
her home.
I am her safety, a dragon,
curling around her, strong,
and warm.

She will run on dirt paths,
and know the faerie homes.
She will feel the monsters,
lurking, and smile a their moonstone eyes,
as they flash in the night.
Her feet will feel
dirt, and twig, and needle.
She'll known no less,
than the extraordinary God breathed around her.
She'll wear dew,
pearled on spider webs around her neck.
She'll have leaves in her hair.
She'll be raw,
and make happiness within
the soil of one hand, and
the moss of the other.

I will continue to create,
and show the creation of magic,
within such tiny hands,
tiny hearts.

I've yet to decide how this will end,
but I know it will end,
and that I will have earned my rest.
I know I wish to be stowed away,
beneath the mountains.
Buried in that fog. That rain. Those paths.
I know my stars will have burned out,
my dreams full, fulfilled,
and twinkling in the fading of my existence.

I will have no less.

So,
I suppose I have decided how this will end.

And I'd better,
work harder.

Thirteen

Inspiration is such demon.
It sits there, on your shelf,
telling you to do everything
your heart desires.

And telling your heart,
you can,
too.

It gives wings.
It gives paths.
It gives opportunities.

It's not until you pet
the demon,
do you know,

it was your heart all along.

Fourteen

I wield words like magic.
Sometimes dainty
and polite.
Sometimes wicked
and warm.
Sometimes beastly
and coated with teeth.

It's all in the move of your soul,
darling.
It's all in the strength of
your weapon.
The tool you pick up
and swing overhead.
Magic can be anything that kindles you.

Like music from fingertip
and breath.
A body bent from dance
and poise.
Hands smudged in charcoal
and pastels.
A warrior's stance
and the years spent there.

Magic is anything that kindles you, darling.

Use it well.

Fifteen

20

Blades made out of stardust
are both the most beautiful
and the most deadly.

They can kill nothing
but dreams.

Sixteen

Those pieces inside rage
like blood loss.
Leaving me pale and
weak.

They thunder on.
Sweeping over mountain scapes and
shifting land that tumble
down.

Those pieces are jagged.
I cut my knees on them
as I pray.

They're dark,
but quiet, at least.

I can feel them all there,
sitting heavy in my chest.
They weigh me down by my very soul.
I know I'll breathe easy,
laying on the floor, exhausted,
once it's all done, and again my mind is
still.

Yet I stand among the chaos.

I watch,
as they don't care what they do,
but only that they have the power
to do.

I bang at the layers.
They crumble one at a time.
All the mud, they've built around me,
and my home.

I'll be standing there in the center.
Sword at the ready.
I'll stand there and tell them this is where they
stop.
They may not bring their chaos here.
This is my land.
This is my land.

It will no longer be my blood,
but theirs.
Their knees will be raw, as they kneel before me,
wide eyes staring up.
This darkness, I'll give it back.
It always belonged to them.

I'll have a scar.
It will run white across my rib.
I see it there some days.

Some days I won't notice at all.
I'll smile on without remembering
the fight.

I'll go on,
treading through the mountains as rain comes,
and I am anew.

I'll go on,
as I kneel and pray,
a pillow below me.

I'll go on,
blowing out my lamp,
and nesting into the darkness.

Some days, I will see it, oh yes.

A reminder,
I feed no one with the smile of the fox.
Not the crumbs from my table, not the water of
my well.
A reminder
that I stood on my threshold, and pointed a
sword
like a curse.
A reminder
of what I paid to know I achieved

happiness.

Seventeen

25

I want to be hung

in sin and grace

reflecting light inward

like a stained glass window.

Eighteen

It's not always moonbeams

and open nights.

But sometimes the sky is clear

and cool

and sometimes

you can see your dreams coming true

in the darkness

between

the stars.

....

I was harvesting the stars one day,
and I saw a pretty face.
It's glisten was of moonbeams,
and it had a frosted taste.

It poisoned me like apples,

silver on their skin.
I drink it in,
the fun begins,
and know what darkness dapples.

I was harvesting the stars one day
and I saw a pretty path.
Milky in its way,
I took a cooling bath.

It led me to a river,
it fell upon the stone.
I walked alone,
back to home,
my cottage warmed with timber.

I was harvesting the stars one day
and a pretty diamond shown so bright.
I danced beneath the belt,
like a witch within the night.

28

Mothers don't just create life
they create souls.

Remember that.

The mother was gentle and easy. The father, strong and open.

Together they created six children.

These children grew in love and grace.

They grew in loud laughter, in dirt, in a warmth only created in homemade bread and oil lamps.

The eldest, he was raised to be strong and proud of who he was. He was raised to love in a way that was deep, and long. Like a Shakespearian tragedy, he left with trails of music.

The second, she was raised with a heart of song. She was raised with a spine. Sturdy, and smart. Proud of who she became, she lacked the will to wither. Instead, she grew with justice and strength.

The third, something gentle came here. She was created out of flower beds. Wild hair and a smile in the wind, she grew to love equally as beautiful children. Her gentleness learned the inside of hearts.

The fourth, he chose no path. No picket fence to box him in. He wondered, loving each thing he learned. Sparks in his eyes drew him to the next journey, and he grew with a love of the world.

The fifth, she was born in words. She scribbled down her stories, tapped them along a typewriter, and spread them around her like blankets. She grew in acceptance, and understanding of those around her. She grew strong and quiet.

The last, she still grows. Something in her wild, and yet longing for the simplicity. She grows in an abundance of pride for her. She grows in the Lord's hand. She grows in those before her.

And what a beautiful forest they make, all growing together as they do.

....

Mother

You may not know it.
But I adore you.
I adore what you have created with nothing but your heart.
I adore that you are
embedded in me.
That I see pieces of you
here.
In my home.

I adore that you are
here, in how I raise
my own.
I adore that you've given
the sharp pieces,
a smooth finish.
I adore most,
that you helped craft me.
That I am, who I am,
in part,
because of you.

You may not know it.
But I adore you.

....

Trees will always be the way I think of you.
The smell of cut wood.
The forest and an abundance of plants and
animals.
A burning fire, with logs you split.

You will always be there,
in the grains of my heart.

....

Sisters

I didn't know your soul could feel that too.
How amazing that is.
That we are so different
and we are so the same.

....

You will never know the strength you have
shown me.
You will never know that my successes

are partly yours.

....

I know you by your boots.
They way they shift through the grass as you
walk.
I know you by a head of wild hair.
I know you by the way I used to hold your hand.
I used to spin you in circles to make you dizzy,
and send you walking.
I used to rub dandelions on your cheeks, to make
them yellow.
I used to catch lightning bugs with you, and
watch them in our jars.
I used to share a bed with you. Your knees
digging into my back.

I miss every bit that you used to be.

And yet, I am filled with such pride of who you
are
today.

....

The Cousin

You-
You are just as close as a sister.
You are just as warm as a friend.
But you possess this wildness,
this unapologetic strength.
And I hope you know, I love that will of yours.
I love the way you take what's been coming,
and you make it your own.
You breathe deep,
some days you cry,
you and feel like you've
shattered.
But still you rise,
and I thank you for it.
For every moment of unconditional love.
For every evening of laughter filled memories.
For every time I fill with pride,
for your successes.
Know I am proud of you.

Know if you are ever alone, you are mine,
and you have a place with me.
Know I hold you dearly.
Know you are a part of my family and
I could not fathom being without you.
You are everything I am not.
And thank you
for loving me as I am.
And thank you,
for the times,
where I am with you,
and I find my center,
without ever having realized
I was off.

Twenty-One

Don't lead gentle
into this place.

Lead with the fires
of your brothers behind you.

Lead with the children
of your sisters with you.

Lead with the forges
of your parents inside you.

Lead with the kiss
of your husband on your mouth.

Lead with your child
on your back.

Lead with your sword
on your hip.

And don't.

Lead.

Gentle.